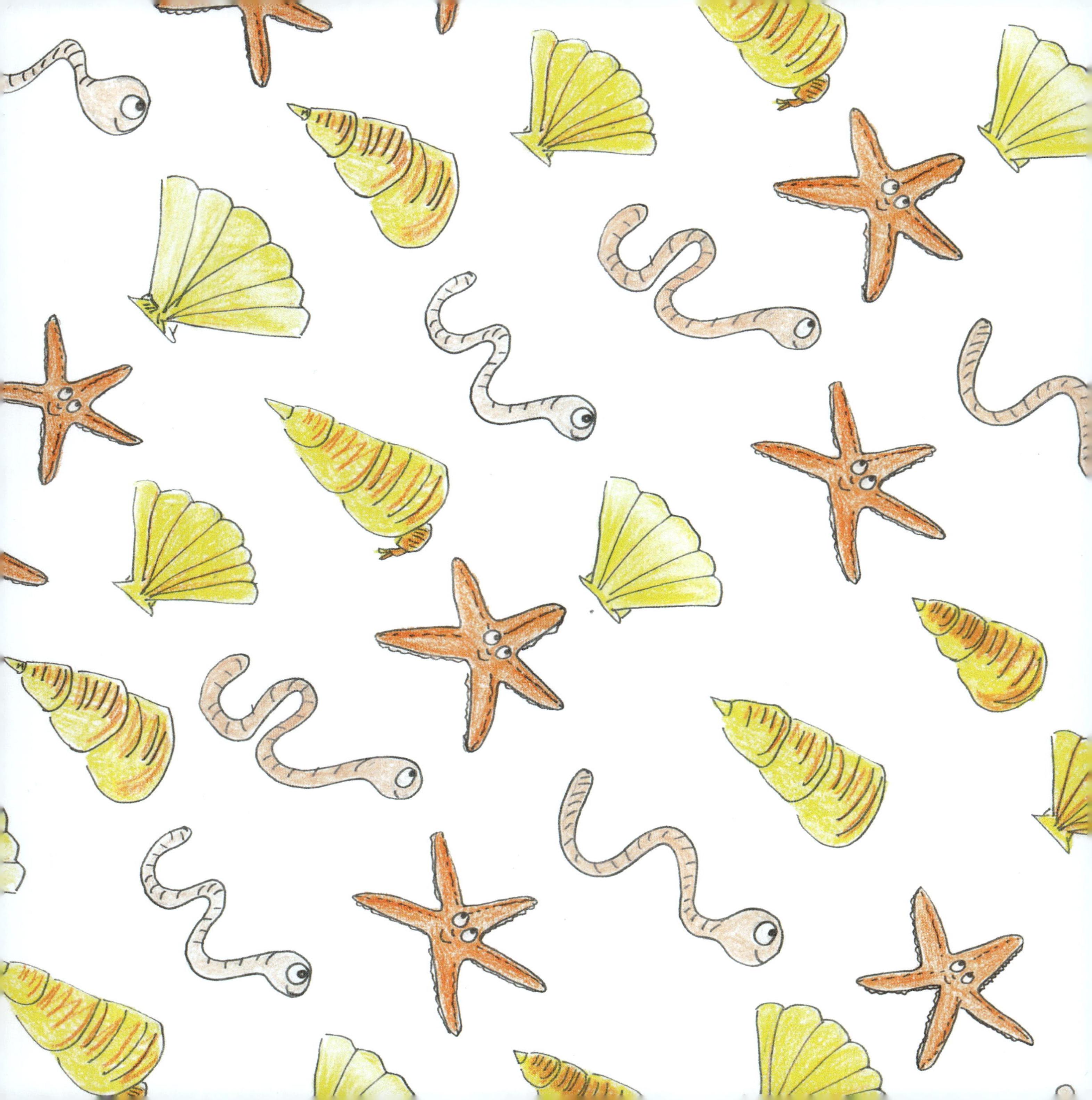

# Pip is a clever little Plover bird

written & illustrated by
Angharad Owen

© 2019 Angharad Mair Owen

To My Family
I'm so blessed and lucky to have them.
Their encouragement has brought me to this point
and their love is the inspiration for this story'

Pip is a clever little Plover bird

he loves...

eating worms

running

and asking QUESTIONS...

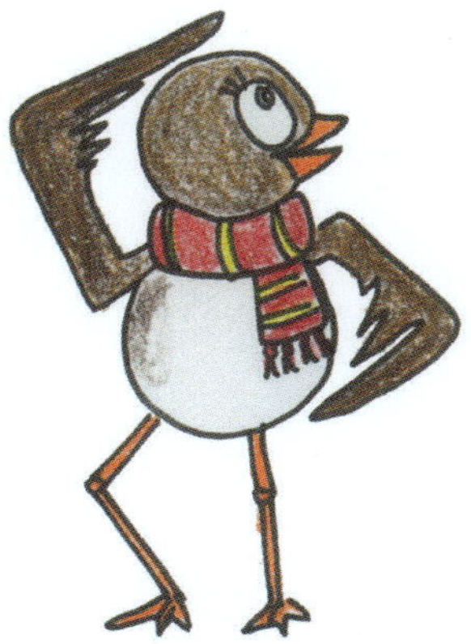

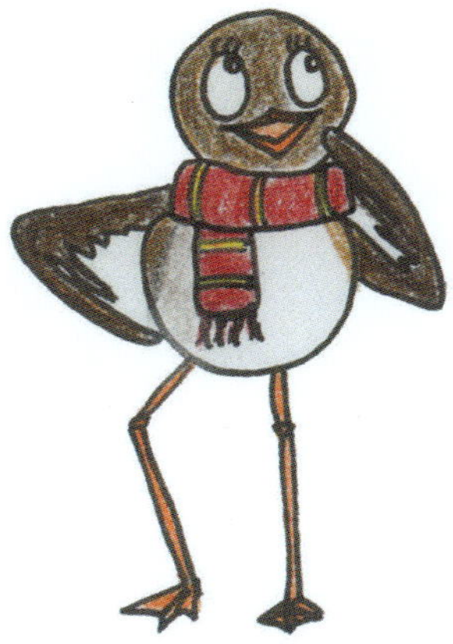

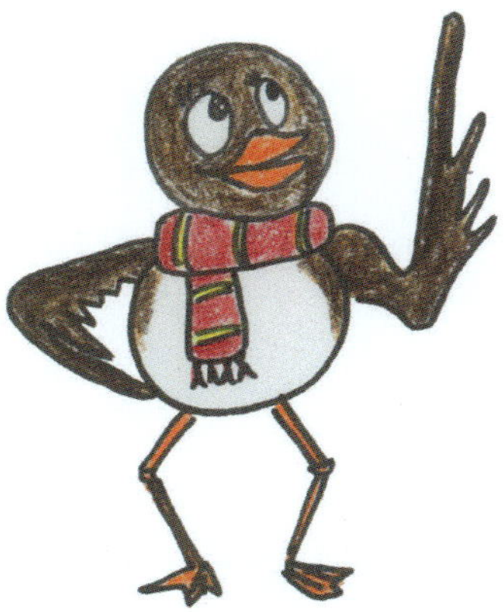

- Why is the sky blue?

- How can I fly?

- Why can't I stay up late?

every day, his family tell him that they love him very much

which made him think...

the one question he has never found the answer to is...

## what is love?

...he wanted to start asking his friends

Suddenly, one of the pebbles on the beach starts to rattle!

if you ask me, feeling safe and protected is love

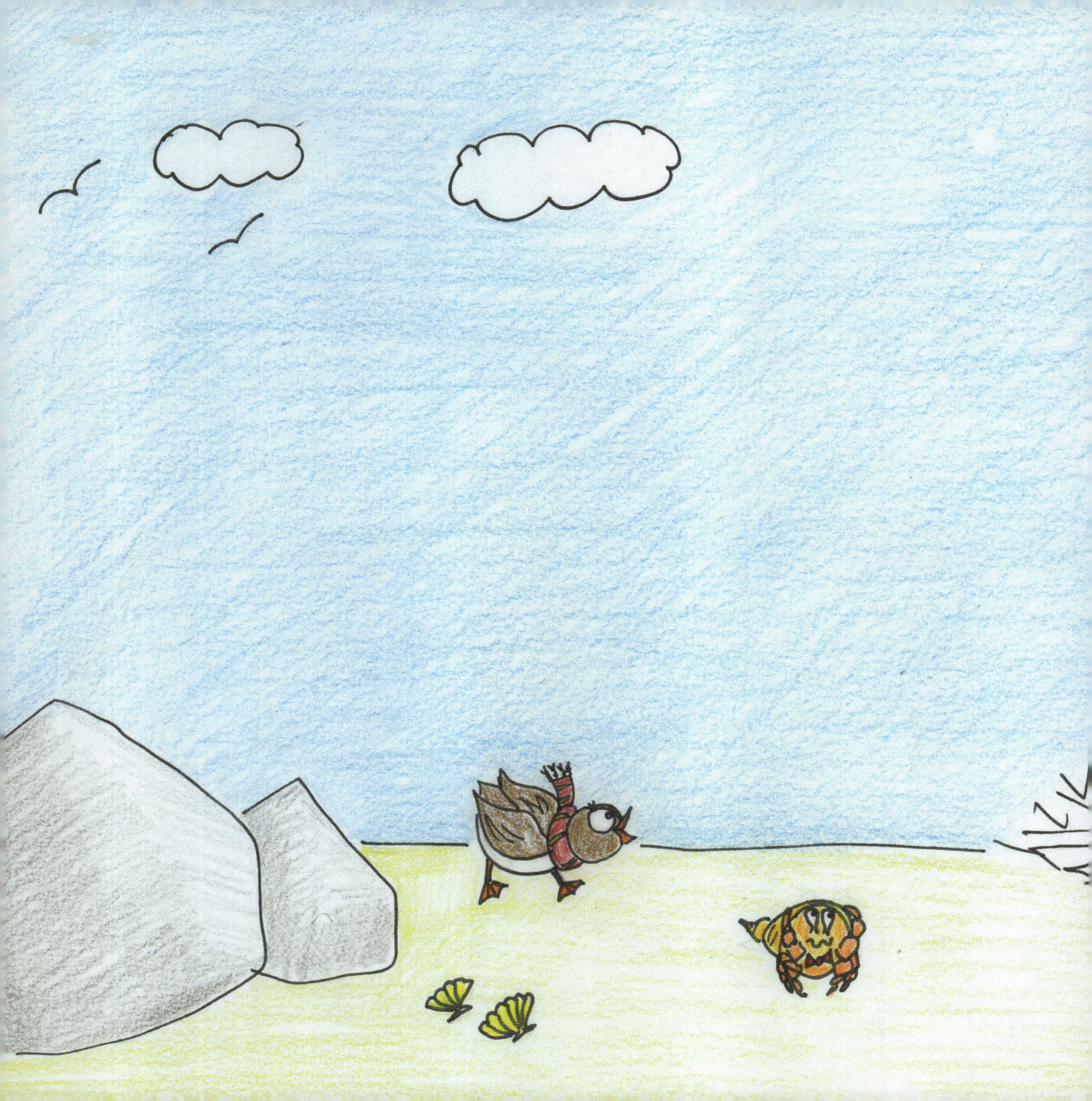

then a huge shadow swooped over...

It was a Heron!

sharing and being kind is love

Pip splashed into the sea to ask the mackerel

Looking after each other and enjoying being together is love.

Pip had to catch his breath and saw seals at the surface!

Love makes you smile and feel happy, they said,

as they flipped and danced in the sea

then from high up on the cliff top - he saw Puffins!

Having a loyal friend you never want to leave, is love

Pip started to think about what everyone had said...

feeling safe & protected

Sharing and being kind

Enjoying being together

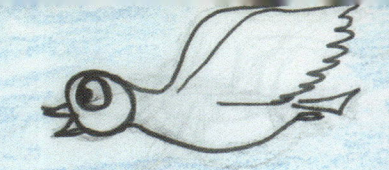

I __have__ all of these things!

he was loved!
And loved them very much

He needed to tell his family.

He started running as fast as he could!

We try to show you how we love you through the things we do!

That's the answer to that question, but I have so many other questions!

Why is the sky blue? Can I stay up late? Why can birds fly?

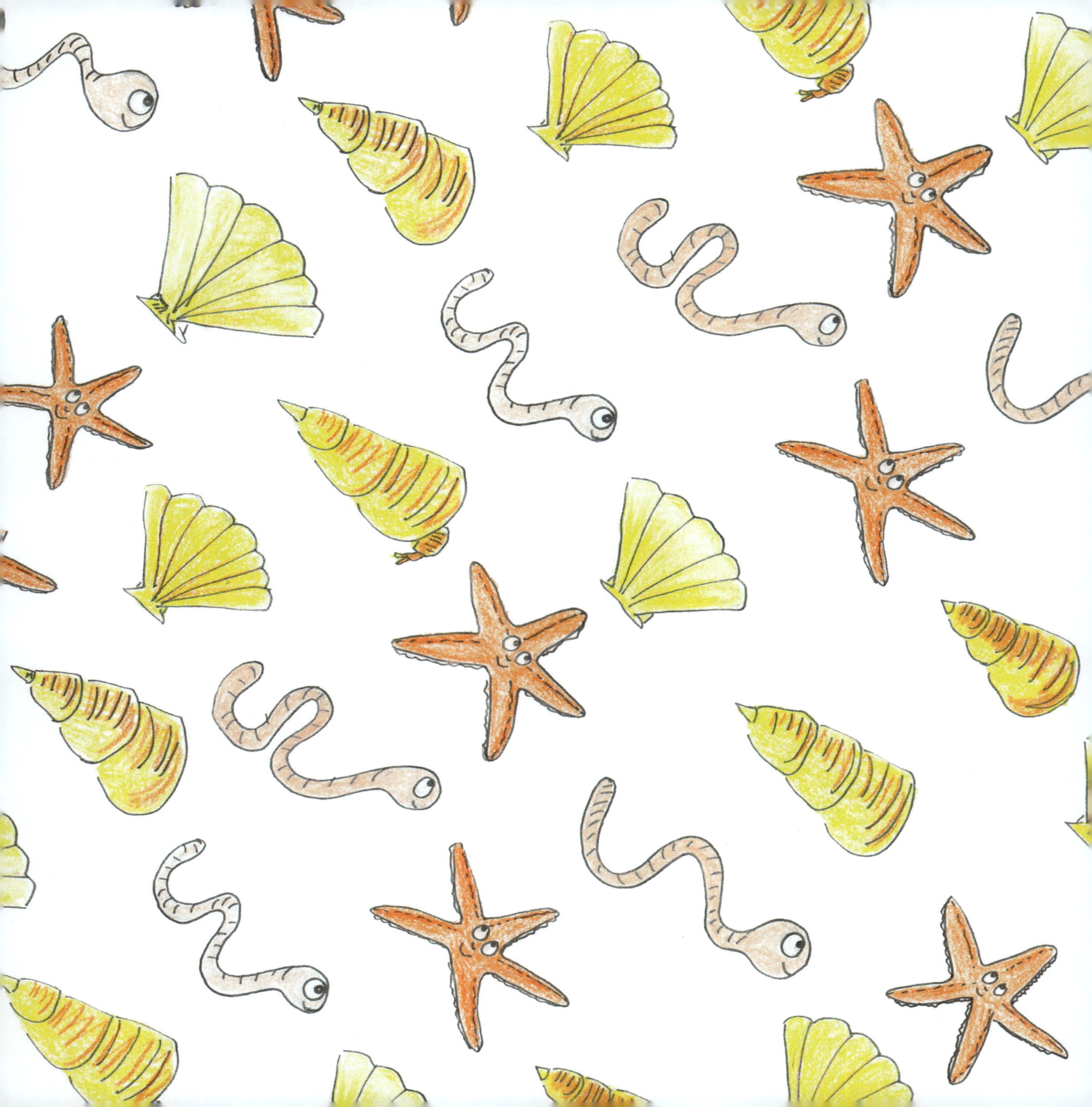

Printed in Great Britain
by Amazon